The Light
AND DARK
of My Mind

by

Rohlan Sulvar

DORRANCE
PUBLISHING CO
EST. 1920
PITTSBURGH, PENNSYLVANIA 15238

Dorrance Publishing Co
585 Alpha Drive
Suite 103
Pittsburgh, PA 15238
Visit our website at *www.dorrancebookstore.com*

ISBN: 978-1-6853-7167-8
eISBN: 978-1-6853-7710-6

NOTES

Welcome to my mind.

Today I will be taking you on a trip through the light and dark side of my mind.

I will show my most inner thoughts,

through my style of writing and my experiences through my life.

Some side notes:

(Put something uncaring, but meaningful here.)

This is for entertainment only. Don't take my words to heart.

Now that we have this settled, please enjoy the ride and I thank you for your time.

SIMPLE SPOKEN WORDS

Move forward
Don't back track
What's done is done
You can't change the past
The brokenness won't last... forever
Accept all that has happened
Forgiveness to yourself
Is the way to go
You're not the only one
Pain and suffering
Loves the agony
Of one's own misery

Don't run away
Stand your ground
Even when you feel like drowning
Echoing through the silence of sound
Don't hold back
When you scream into the night
When you refuse to flight
Shine so bright
In all your light

Let go of all your shame
Don't take what you're not to blame
It's not your time for this fame
We are not the banes

✿✿✿

ROHLAN SULVAR

INNOCENCE OF THE GUILTY

I've tried to look on the brighter side
Even when my demons hide
After the shadows begin to collide
Racing to my final ride
To reach your stars
Bottling up my hidden scars

Lying next to you
I swear this is true
For the things you do
Healing my broken mind
I would walk the line

Mending my cracking soul
Closing down
Don't let me drown
When they bury me underground?
Under the fall sky

Save and help me
To find who I need to be
My heart's come undone
How did I
Become so stray
From your path built for me

I can't live a lie
Break down and cry
Set me free
From my sins within me
Who am I supposed to be?
Lying next to you
I swear this is true
For all the things you do
Healing my aching mind
For you do I swear
I will walk that line

The blood-stained walls
As I'm spinning circles
Down your forbidden halls
Reaching out before I
Take the fall
Craving it all.

✿ ✿ ✿

ROHLAN SULVAR

HIDDEN GEM

I can see
See the stars
Shining in your eyes
Even with all the scars
The scars you hide behind
All will be fine
Once you begin to shine
In the night sky
To the heavens high
Climbing on cloud nine
Dragged down
By the shadow's past
This pain won't ever last
Let go of everything
Wipe the slate clean
Nothing is ever as it seems
Gazing through the star beams
Floating through
Time and space
This was never meant to be a race
Ghosting without a trace
Grasping the light of grace
Shifting through the many faces
Walk the line
Between the dark and light
Holding onto what you fear
Voices so unclear
That can be heard
Echo through the winds
You will find your happiness

❀❀❀

DO YOU EVEN CARE?

Would you walk away?
If I spoke the truth
Would you walk away?
If I confess my love for you
Would you turn around?
If my screams echo without a sound

Do you even care?
That I bled for you
Do you even care?
That I willingly sacrifice
My life for you
Do you even care?
After all I've done for you
If I end it all
Took the fall

Shut me out
Cold shoulder
Dead zone
Silencing my echo
Left behind
To your empty mind

Do you even care?
If I bled for you
Do you even care?
That I willingly sacrifice
My life for you.
Do you even care?
After all I've done for you
If I end it all
Took the fall.

Don't you dare
Speak ill of me
Behind closed doors
Don't you dare
Put the blame
Back on me

Do you even care?

✿✿✿

A PAST THAT HAUNTS

My shadows surround me
Spinning circles around what comes to be
As my demons drown what I see
Never realizing how it fails
Floating away in your dreams
Becoming just a nightmare

The tortures I played
Pain and suffering you felt
All the mental scars
I gave you through the years
Insecure of all my fears
Caught up from my lies

Walk away from everything
Just to leave me to my sins
Never learning from where I've been
As I rage my wars within
Just to feel my heartstrings come undone
Please don't pray for me
Stray away from me

I crossed the line
Shattered and broken your mind
Never claiming that you were mine
Always leaving you behind
I was blind to see
What was becoming of me?
Please accept my apologies
For all my sinful crimes
For all the scars I gave

❀❀❀

WATCH ME BURN

Set me aflame
To watch me burn
At the stake again
As you put the blame (on me)
This was never my destiny
For your blind to see

Believe in your lies
For that's your truth
At night your cries
Reach the skies
The heavens won't hear
They sense your fear
Visions become hazy and unclear

Enter my nightmares
Tormented souls and mind
Are you brave enough?
To survive my fairy tale fables
I am willing and able
Lay it all on the line
The cards are on the table

Set me a flame
To watch me burn
At the stake again
As you put the blame (on me)
This was never my destiny
For your blind to see

Can you feel it in your heart?
Breaking as the world falls apart
Losing your only way through the dark
Blinded by sight
Lost all your light
No will left to fight
I am your blight

Feel me in your veins
I've become your hated bane
Haunting your surviving sanity
Insane aren't we all?
Climb the walls
To drop for the long fall
All away down
I'll watch you drown
In my wasting sorrows
Hollow and shallow

Set me aflame
To watch me burn
At the stake again
As you put the blame on me
This will never be my destiny
For your blind to see

❁❁❁

THE DREAM NIGHTMARE

I've been running, running
Running through the dark
I've been chasing, chasing
Chasing after my stolen heart
I've been watching, watching
Watching you fall apart
Broken and damage
Cruel cold world, savage
Bear to walk the line
All alone to find
What was once deep inside
Bury it all to hide
When did I become so blind?
That you were fading
In front of me
I couldn't see
That I was being torn open
For you to feast upon
My flesh and soul
Leave me to die
Don't you dare cry
For me
Hands reaching for the sky
Time for me to fly
Leaving you to your lies

❀❀❀

RETURN TO HIS LIGHT

Shadows of the dark
I stroll through the park
Just to calm my bleeding heart
Trying to silence the echoing
Of my demon's bark
The racing in my brain
Panicking as I drown
In the pouring rain
As it all becomes circling in the drain
Blocking out the sounds

Facing, confronting my crimes of sin
Fighting from the deep within
Where it all begins
Here I go again
Doesn't matter where I've been
Just to make amends
As everything starts to spin
Falling to my knees
I beg you please
Save me
From whom I use to be

I was who I was
Didn't have a care in the world
Hurting the ones that truly cared
About me
I was blinded by the false desires
Lusting after all the wild fires
Breaking every commandment placed before me
Failing to see
Who truly loved me
I became the ship wreck
Upon your shore

I wanted to end it all
Jump and take that fall
Running back and forth in the halls
Corridors of the cracking walls
Clean slate, reborn flesh
I am a new

Facing, confronting my crimes of sin
Fighting from deep within
Where it all began
There I go again
Doesn't matter where I've been
Just to make amends
As everything starts to spin
I beg you please
Save me, from who I use to be

✿✿✿

I AM

Flames and ashes
I've taken my beatings
My slashes
Broken and tortured
But I climbed and crawled
Just to rise to the top

Spit your lies
Drag me through the mud
To all your demons and devils
I've reaped what I've sown
Admitting to what I've always known
I will become your social hazard
Riding out the blizzard

Haunt my nightmares
Torment my dreams
For I won't hear your screams
My silence will echo your violence
Am I making it clear?
I no longer fear

I have a reason to fight
Are you strong enough?
To with stand my light
Spread my healing wings
Take flight
I won't be your bane
I am beyond my shame
Suffer in the falling rain

ROHLAN SULVAR

I am
What your fear most
I am
The rising of my fallen ghost
I am
The man of many healed scars

✿✿✿

BEYOND YOU

This is not your time
Don't cross that line
Regardless if you get left behind
Because you have so much
Left to shine!

Beaten and broken down
Let those who drown you
Fall into their own hell
Rise above what they make you
You are truer than you see
Don't be afraid of your tears
Cry it out
Don't fear or have that doubt

Surrounded by your darkness
That's okay if you rebel and misbehave
Just don't feel like your worthless
I must confess
I walked in your boots
For fourteen years
I've rode the waves
Passion fires, darken desires
Those your secretly admire
I was a loaded gun for hire

Look beyond the silence
Echoing in the winds of violence
Rise above the ashes and flames
Forgive your past shames
Let go of the blames

✿✿✿

ROHLAN SULVAR

FALLING FROM THE SKIES

Shooting stars
Wishing to heal
Your showing scars
Shooting stars
Wishing to just
Fade away
Becoming a forgotten memory

Drowning from your sins
Reliving your crimes
Of your past
Submit to your demons
Torments of your own hell
Forgetting that you fell

Look into my eyes
Go beyond the tears shed
See that I speak no lies
Don't draw back
I won't say good-bye
My how the times flies
Fall from the skies

Don't lose sight
Pray, hope, and fight
We are all a blight
Stay with me
Come back to the light
Let's take this flight

Abuse and rape
The hate we feel
Bruised and battered
The scars we've become
Alcohol and pills
Feeling dull and numb
Fall all the way back down

Run and hide
The battles
Of war left inside
Swimming past the tide
Of our lives

Look into my eyes
Go beyond the tears shed
See that I speak no lies
Don't draw back
I won't say good-bye
My how the times flies
Fall from the skies

✿✿✿

THE FIRST OF MY NIGHTMARES

Break me down
Watch me drown
Then bury me beneath
Beneath the sinking ground
Just to get me out of the way
Because of your heart's sway
Fly away
To the setting sun
We've only just begun

Hang me
From your wilting tree
Just to set yourself free
Never falling to your knees
What will never become of me
To the worlds may be
You have become so blind to see

Collapsing in on yourself
Losing everything
Right before your eyes
As it seems you begin
Choking on all your lies
Begging for my help
Don't you dare cry
Don't you dare shed a single tear
As my time grows near
Becoming in death what you fear
To leave you all behind

THE LIGHT AND DARK OF MY MIND

I build my walls
To keep you out
I fail to fall
Breaking your every doubt
You've lied about
You want me to feel
Yourself suffering

I won't bring myself
Down to your level
My broken heart won't sway
To fall apart
I've shed my tears
Crying alone in the dark

Knowing that you're suffering
Alone you break
I cannot feel for you
Anymore

✿✿✿

ROHLAN SULVAR

THE PLAGUE OF NIGHTMARES

Alone
Left to my demons
Haunting from within
The darkness in
My broken mind
Chain me to the walls
Deep in my sins
Falling closer to
My own hell

I burn
Burn to ask
Pain screaming
Echoing through silence
Life with no sound
I've begun to drown
Sinking my lost soul
Beneath the ground

Fade away
To the place I
Dare not want to go
I'm holding on
By this thin line
I refuse to obey
Accepting what I may
Become to be

THE LIGHT AND DARK OF MY MIND

Abusive bruising
My agony rages
Through my skull
Numb and dull
I can't lose it all
Covered in all your scars

No matter what I do
I can't look beyond
To a better day
Drowning in my ways
I collapse like
A broken tainted heart
Blinded in my darkness

Torment my soul
Visions of sugar plum demons
Haunt my sleeping mind
Dancing in the calming fires
Fueling my false desires

✿✿✿

TO THE START

Rip out my eyes
So I can't see your lies
Shedding blood to cry
This will be my last good-bye
My end is nigh
As the world gets high
Take to the sky

Seal me away
Forever willing
Just to fade
Becoming another of your strays
Whatever comes my way
I cannot obey

Willing and able
Spinning your fable
Sharks under your table
Under the sky so blue
Nothing was ever true
Spoken words from you
Of the actions you do

Night of the falling stars
Where my scars
Shine so bright
In the moon's light
Fading in the distance
In the blink of my existence
Finding treasures we seek
Just above the winter's peek
Seal me away
Forever willing
Just to fade
Becoming another of your strays
Whatever comes my way
I cannot obey

Leave me to the dark
Alone with my mending heart
Crying and screaming
As my world falls apart
Returning to the start

❀❀❀

SLOWLY BACK TO THE LIGHT

I fell in love
Within the darkness I found
Chain and torture
My soul became bound
My world I had
Began to drown
Into the seas underground

Like an angel falling from grace
I've became what I hated most
Refusing to be a man and face
I've became a shell, a fading ghost
Gone without a trace
Down the rabbit's hole
Following false desires
Giving up on my hearts hope

Who am I
Screaming without the echoing
Blind to see
That you never gave up on me
I fall to my knees
Help me
Become who I need to be
Bring back the light
For I shall begin
To break my chains and fight
Even in the darkness you show
I still have my sight

Forgiveness you gave
For my crimes of sin
Regardless of my demons within
Doesn't matter where I been
The future of your love
Is all I shall crave
Fighting to what's right

I have crossed the line
Too many times
Always on a thin line
Searching for pleasures
That was never mine
My war rages on
Inside my dying mind
Please don't leave me behind
Lost within my mind

✿✿✿

THE KNIGHT

Born of royal blood
For the greater good
Tested to be the sacrifice
To save those they don't know
Of the void take in the radiance
But you came so close

Trapped forever along with the rest
So how you escape, your will alone
You followed your own path
To walk alone
Eventually making your way back home
No memories
To remember where you came from
Fighting your way
Enduring everything that may come
Helping those with ever few words
Being guided by those who have seen
Your strength deep inside
Saving those who would reject you
Who would cast you aside?
But holding true to never hide

Proving to yourself
Those around you
You are indeed the savior
Long forgotten
Nail in hand
Fearless to face your destiny
To face a reality of destruction
Long kept away from the world
Courage of the fallen outcast

THE LIGHT AND DARK OF MY MIND

Hollow suffering
Sorrow pain
Throw it all away
Nothing was ever gain
As our memories fade
Sane or insane
Taking it to our graves
Cutting deep to the veins

Void of darkness
Flicker of out dying light
Trying to remember
The happier of times
As we lay
In the cooling shade

Move on forward
Stepping backwards
Never knowing where to go
Floating in the river
Going where the current
Takes us in our mind
Following lust or desires
Of the aching heart
Before our world falls apart

Being loved
Having loved
Spoken so easy
To those who have

ROHLAN SULVAR

Been through hell
Who have fell
Surpassing the trails
We are what we are
Beyond societies expectations

✿✿✿

BEAUTY IN YOUR DARKNESS

There is beauty
Within your darkness
Hidden behind your eyes
Regardless of the lies,
You believe
I know you're not worthless

Trials of the mistakes
We've all made
Has left a shadow void
To our darker selves
Excuses to end out lives
But we are stronger
Than we are led to see
What we are meant to be

Look beyond my soul
See the truth I hold
Trust me when I say

There is beauty
Within your darkness
Hidden behind your eyes
Regardless of the lies,
You believe
I know you're not worthless

Hollow empathy
Towards the ones we love
Apathy of sorrow

Don't phase me at all
As you scramble to climb your walls
As the worlds falls

Tainted and Shattered
Broken by are dreams
Nothing is as it seems
Echoing our screams
With no sound
Tearing at the seams

Look beyond my soul
See the truth that lies
Trust me when I say

There is beauty
Within your darkness
Hidden behind your fading eyes
Regardless of the lies,
You believe
I know the truth within you

✿✿✿

MY WORDS

Stepping into the shadows
The void of my darkness
Where my flickering light
Begins to slowly fade
Sit around my life
Recasting of my tales
Forgetting the happier times
Filling me with all your lies

Watch me die
Throw me to the shade
As my flame sways
To the echoes of my agony
Melody to twisted ears
Recast my tainted soul
My cracking heart
Laughing as I fall apart

Bury me deep underground
To the apathy of those around
Echoing no of sound
For no love surrounded me
I was never who I was meant to be
Blinded by those who can see

Stepping in the shadows
The void of my darkness
Where my flickering light
Begins to slowly fade
Sit around my fire
Recasting of my tales
Forgetting the happier times
Filling me with all your lies

I am no candle,
But I feel my wick getting low
I no longer
Have the will to fight
Just to become another
One of the blights
Beyond my dying sight
I was always right

✿✿✿

RESTING GROUNDS

My time has come
My end is drawing near
I have been through ten thousand worlds
Over one thousand life times
Replaying every battle in my head
Fading light
Losing fight
This everlasting blight

Take me to the resting grounds
Where the silence is sound
In death I grow stronger
My flame won't last much longer
To the depths below
Devouring shadows
Give me my final round

Bold and proud
Crowds cheering
So loud
Champions from around the world
To be the best of the best
Almost time for the final test
Holding onto my crest
Clashing of nails
I can never fail

Take me to the resting grounds
Where the silence is sound
In death I grow stronger
My flame won't last much longer
To the depths below
Devouring shadows
Give me my final round

My scars have only shown
What I secretly known
Slicing to break the bones
For my life had purpose
As your end, no meaning
Born of the blacken void

Take me to the resting grounds
Where the silence is sound
In death I grow stronger
My flame won't last much longer
To the depths below
Devouring shadows
Give me my final round

Take me to the resting grounds
Where the silence is sound
In death I grow stronger
My flame won't last much longer
To the depths below
Devouring shadows
Give me my final round

✿✿✿

AS OUR ENERGY FLOWS

I see your fiery soul
The burning desire in your eyes
I can feel the passion in your heart
When I hold you close
I see the flame burning bright
When I look at your beauty
In the darkness you show
As our energy flows

To the stars and worlds beyond
As we watch the night sky
Wishing for this to never end
Dare I be so bold
To take your hand to hold
As my nightmares fade away
To your shining melodies I sway
Only to stay
Just to keep the demons at bay

Day goes by
As your beauty shines
Like the stars
No need to hide your scars
You calm the storms
That rages from within me
As I ease your pain and suffering
Torture souls and tainted hearts
Never to fall apart
Alone in the dark

ROHLAN SULVAR

I'll wipe away your tears
So, you will hear
My words to become clear
I'll hold onto you my dear
Let go of the fears
You hide
For I will fight at your side
I will never leave
You behind

I know your fiery soul
I've felt the burning desire
From your eyes
I've seen the passion within
Your heart
I've never let go of you
Your never fading flame
Burning ever so brightly
I know you're beyond beautiful
Your true light shows
As our energy flows

THE MEMORIES

Staring off
To the setting sun
Fading away
Beyond the horizon
Lost to my thoughts
As I breath to the winds
Carry my echoes

Fall back to the ground
Silences comes
To the dying sounds
Staring off
To the coming stars
Lost within my mind
Lost to time
Where did it all go?

I remember the memories
That we never made
I remember the times
That we never shared
I remember my darkness
That you were never there
I remember

I wake in the pouring rain
Numb to the freezing cold
To the everlasting pain
Shattering my cracking heart
What did I hope to gain?
When my world came
Falling apart

Mix signals
Came in clear
Fading lights
I've come to fear
Lost without a fight
No one was here
I am machine
I cannot hear

I remember the memories
That we never made
I remember the times
That we never shared
I remember my darkness
That you were never there
I remember

Falling tears
To my fading echoes
Losing it all
Soaking wet
What is truly I fear?
My love for you
I won't remember
I won't remember you

✿✿✿

WHY DO YOU?

Why do you run away?
From all the good
That's right in front of you
Why do you run away?
From those that keep
Your shadows at bay
No matter what may come

Leap out to the fade
As your broken heart sways
Why do you leave us all behind?
When you fall to the white lines?
Assuming all will be fine
What answers do you hope to find?
In the emptiness of your mind

Daring and bold
Does your fading soul,
Ever fold?
Making everyone your nameless fool
Look beyond the setting sun
Just to behold
There is no beauty
In the tales your told

Swallow the pills
Just to fill
Your emptiness of hope
Drink until
It all comes crashing down
But your emotions flood
To those who don't hold still

ROHLAN SULVAR

Why do you run away?
From all the pain
Left bury buried inside
Why do you run away?
From everything you hold in vane
What do you hope to gain?
Slicing deep into the veins

✿✿✿

I'VE GIVEN UP ON YOU.

I've been down this road
Way too many times before
And now here we are again
Why do I let you do this to me?
How have I
Become so blind to see
To whom you really are
I've lost count on
How many scars,
You left on me

Slowly I fall behind
Just to watch you fade away
Hoping one day you'll look back
To see if I'm still following
But I've chose to walk
A different line
Knowing my soul won't be fine
Becoming a part of
The lost and never found
Do my own thoughts echo
To your fading heart beat sound

Cut myself to feel the pain
Dwelling memories of you linger
Though nothing is ever gain
I'm slowly losing my brain
As my rage goes insane
I've taken it all in vane

I've given up on you my friend
I've come to the end
I can no longer bend
To your unspoken rules
I've killed all lights
Sever all lines
Cutting all ties that bind
Letting it all drown
Shattering my glass heart
I'm down falling apart
Back to the shadows
Where you left me to the dark

I've been down this road before
Way too many times before
And now here we are again
Why do I let you do this to me?
How have I
Become so blind to see
To who you really are
I've lost count on
How many scars,
You left on me

Fade away
To the hollow shade
I cannot stay
To how you sway
Keeping my feelings at bay

✿✿✿

OF MY SINS

The night echoes
Through the winds
Silence beckons
The darkness gravity
Pulls me in
From within

Facing the rage
Of my sins
Burning the unwanted
Bridges never crossed
Just to be forgotten
By the pretending
Of my friends
I won't apologize
To bring it all to an end

So long my fading light
My dying star
I will forever
Embrace the un-healing scars
I won't put up a fight
To the unforgiving shadows
Out of the pacing mind's sight
Never going far

The night echoes
Through the winds
Silence beckons
The darkness gravity
Pulls me in
From within

Leave me behind
Throw me off the line
My Heart is lost
It won't shine
Toss it to the void
Torture my soul
Tainted and twisted
Shatter my dreams
To your reality of nightmares
Just to fill your
Empty hole

The night echoes
Through the winds
Silence beckons
The darkness gravity
Pulls me in
From within

The night echoes
Through the winds
Silence beckons
The darkness gravity
Dragging me in
Ripping me apart
From within

✿✿✿

FOR YOU, FROM ME

Sever the ties
That bind
Break the chains
Free my mind
Sight beyond sight
To the lies that blind
Only now do I see
To the truth I find
It was never truly never mine

My heart thrown to
The darken void
Twisted by your
Tainted soul
I've done my best
To hold...... ON!
You were meant to complete me
Make me whole...... again
So now I...

Sever the ties
That bind
Break the chains
Free my mind
Sight beyond sight
To the lies that blind
Only now do I see
To the truth I find
It was truly never mine

Break and shatter
My bones
Demonize your lullabies
Just to paralyze
Froze in time
Mesmerized, hypnotize
Your playful words
Wide awake
So now I…

Find myself at fault
To forever walk
These empty halls
Becoming lost
As I fall away
Begin to fade…
Can somebody wake me
So I can

(x2)
Sever the ties
That bind
Break these chains
Free my mind
Sight beyond sight
To the lies that blind
Only now do I see
To the truth I find
You were never truly mine

✿✿✿

TO WHERE IT BEGINS

My mind draws a blank
As I'm stuck in between
The reality of my world
And the lust of craving you
Just to find the way
Of my words to speak
Never so truer
Shifting through my many
Fantasies that echoes silently
As I chant my unwritten elegy

My mind silences
The raging echoes
Of the whisperings
You leave behind
To follow
When we are by each other's side
I try to hide
What little emotions
That burn and fuel
The desires you bring to life
In my fading heart

I've done my best
To sever the ties
That you try to bind
That makes us blind
To where we all walk
That invisible line
Color coded chalk…

ROHLAN SULVAR

Only to be washed away
To the tide
That begins to rise

Burning passion
The fires grow
In my mending soul
Just to fall all over again
To where it begins
As we fall apart
Right from the start

✿✿✿

DON'T LOOK BACK

You know
I've tried
I've tried my best
Now I have lay it all to rest
Hours go on bye and are gone
A forgotten soul
That I forgot so long ago
There's a soul and it's fightin' to bury me now, now
If I fade away, will you carry me down

Don't look back
There's nothing left to see
Just leave it all in the past
If you let go
Can you forget these emotions?
And with that
Today is gone and we can never get it back
But I can still feel you though
As I wake you from this nightmare

Bring me back to the light
You've kept me in the dark
Visions becoming clear,
You left a mark
On my tainted heart
I'm a fading soul and I won't be forgotten now
If you fade away, I can't carry you down

ROHLAN SULVAR

Don't look back
Don't look back cause,
There's nothing left to see
Just leave it all in the past
If you let me go
Can you forget these emotions?
With that
Today is gone and we can never get it back, back
But I can still feel you though
Please wake me,
Wake me from this nightmare

MEMORIES IN THE RAIN

As the rains fall
I rethink of it all
Everything that has come to pass
A life that was not meant to last
Flooding in the streets of the town
Only in my mind, do they drown

Shadows of reflections
Painful memories
Agony of the destruction
Tainted my dreams
Echoing of an empty scream
Remembering the time ago

In the awake
Of all my mistakes
What lies true,
Are the images of you
The smile of your deceiving eyes
Should've seen your playful lullabies

What was meant to realize
That it became so demonized
When you sung your sweet lies
That I've become so paralyzed
Falling through the darken skies
Into the shadows
Open by the windows
Drowning out the widows
Entering this limbo
How did we get so low?
Let's begin
Que the playing violin
Demons from within
Facing my sins
Empty the bins
Of the lost souls

Shadows of reflections
Painful memories
Agony of the destruction
Tainted my dreams
Echoing of an empty scream
Remembering the time ago

Every memory in the rain
Letting go of all my pain
Nothing can never be gain
As we take it all in vane

✿✿✿

BOUND SLAVE

I am yours for the taking
Feast upon my treasures of flesh
That are never few
Strap me down
Have your way with me
This is what was meant to be

Blind me
So, I can't see
Straddle me and feast upon
Take it all that I have to offer
My mistress
I am your bound slave
Bonded to your will and wishes

Bleed me dry
Drink my blood
Turns me on
Filling and feeding
Our sexual desires
Fantasies of reality
Of my state of hardness

Blind me
So, I can't see
Straddle me and feast upon
Take it all that I have to offer
My mistress
I am your bound slave
Bonded to your will and wishes

Command and demand me
Follow your orders without question
Just your slave
Can't have any hesitation
No misdirection
All the information
Use me
Abuse me
Leaving me till I'm barely breathing

So, I can't see
Straddle me and feast upon
Take it all that I have to offer
My mistress
I am your bound slave
Bonded to your will and wishes

Just your bound slave
I
I will behave
I
I will obey

✿✿✿

YOU'RE PRETENDING

It's safe to say
That you're so fucking sad
Gotta mock and make fun of everyone
But miles away your trying to be like them
It's fucking pathetic how lost you truly are
Drinking at home to chase away the pain
Too scared to show your face
But if the blind lead the blind
Then everyone can see your true colors

But go ahead and give it your best shot
Because I won't go down without a fight
Coming after me with everything you got
Blow for blow, I can take your beating
By the time you're finish,
I'll be the only one still left standing
I could have been the better man and
Walked away
But enough is enough, I'm done being a gentleman
I'll let go of my silence
Trade it in for the violence

Stop trying to pretend to be me
You'll never have the balls
To climb my walls
Take the falls
Just to stand tall
You're too small
To reach my breaking star

No matter how fast you can run
I'll be too far ahead
It's taken me long to get here
My path is still lost within the fog
I'll never make it clear
Left to my shadows
Black out my windows
Only left for the fallen widows

Don't try to see
You'll never find me
I am who I chose to be
I am not your friend
I'll leave you behind
In the end

But go ahead and give it your best shot
Because I won't go down without a fight
Coming after me with everything you got
Blow for blow, I can take your beating
By the time you're finish,
I'll be the only one still left standing
I could have been the better man and
Walked away
But enough is enough, I'm done being a gentleman
I'll let go of my silence
Trade it in for the violence

✿✿✿

THE BREAKING POINT

Floating…
Floating farther away
Till I disappear
Away from you
What was ever said
I was never true

Fragments or figments
Of my imagination
Broken racing mind
I don't know what is real
Body numb,
Cold as ice
Frozen to my hearts core
With the eagles I sore

Crawling and clawing
Unable to break my prison walls
To the bone
Scrapping the flesh and blood
I can hear their whisperings
Coming from all around me

Cracking and breaking
The splintering of my broken bones
Blinding by the lights
One fire
Many desires
I can feel myself began to spiral

Floating…
Floating farther away
Till I disappear
Away from you
What was ever said
I was never true

Crying…
Uncontrollably
I cannot stop
Calling for mother
Refuse medication
Unable to move
Covered in red and white
Everyone is watching me
From the inside my head

✿✿✿

TRIPPING MIND

Racing back and forth
In my shattering mind
As I'm counting the shadows
Looking out the windows
Screaming into the fading echoes
As my world of dreams
Begin to shatter
Ascending levels of your intoxication feels

I'm a failure
In the eyes
Of mending soul
By my involuntary actions
Of my imaginary conversations
For the justifications of
My solitary satisfaction

Floating, floating
Getting higher
Just to sit and watch
My descending white cube
Falling, falling
To the cracking in the sky
As it
Splits right in two

I'm a genius
In my own eyes
Healing a mending soul
By the involuntary actions

Of their imaginary conversations
For their justifications of
Their self-solitary conversations

Chant my eulogy
Feel the empathy
As they cast my sympathy
When the darkness,
Devours the day light

Failure to amending soul
By my involuntary actions
Of my own imaginary conversations
For justifications of
My damming solitary satisfactions

Victims aren't we all

✿✿✿

CHIME THE BELL

Re-spark the fading life
The broken soul
The torn open heart
Stitching the bleeding mind
Reverse the sins from time

Damages to be done
Bite and stay your tongue
Spoken words
Never can be heard
Eyes blind
Tell the sweetest lies
And we all die

Draw the bodies
Of the chalk lines
Wandering souls
Left behind
Are there unspoken words
Coming in clearly

Re-spark the fading life
The broken soul
The torn open heart
Stitching the bleeding mind
Reverse the sins from time

Reaching for a falling star
Just to catch what isn't there
How did we ever get this far?
As well fell apart
In this everlasting dark

ROHLAN SULVAR

Chime the Bell
For those who live
Forgive the shadows on the wall
Beaten and battered
Torn and tattered
The innocence of the mind
Does it really ever matter

Re-spark (x3)
Re-spark the fading life

✿ ✿ ✿

INHALE...

Inhale...
My unspoken words
Exhale...
All your angels and forgiving sins
Take it all
At face value
Forever a slave to
The never changing times

Step into the everlasting darkness
Lit by the burning flames
Reborn in mother's eulogy
Welcome to the new paradise
Suffering the lies of forging truths
Never to escape her delusional

Monsters and demons
Awakening nightmares
Shifting the worlds of reality
Loaded weapons
To combat mass destruction
Of her abstract god
Born from the mother's womb
Child's body of innocence
Splitting her mind and soul

Inhale…
My unspoken words
Exhale…
All your angels and forgiving sins
Take it all
At face value
Forever a slave to
The never changing times

You can face your truths
And end the illusions
Or succumb to lies
That beckons you to follow
Spiraling and drowning
Suffering of your loved ones
Centering your soul right two

Step into the everlasting darkness
Lit by the burning flames
Reborn in mother's eulogy
Welcome to the new paradise
Suffering the lies of forging truths
Never to escape her delusional

Sacrificing the flesh
Of the heart and soul

✿✿✿

FEAST UPON THE

Taste the fear
Make it clear
Can you hear (me)?
Through the echoes
Falling through time and space

Reaching out with my mind .
Evacuate my feelings
Leave me an empty shell
Just to mirror my former self
Pros and cons to live or die
We all can see the past that lies
Shifting through the children's eyes

Feast upon the crawling
But never feed the hunger
Never be thirsty again
Reborn in the imagination
Of figments to the starvation
Lingering and wandering souls
Swimming lost in the hearts
Of the untold
Always unfolding to no future

Taste the fear
Make it clear
Can you hear (me)?
Through the echoes
Falling through time and space

ROHLAN SULVAR

Bathing in the fading sun
Wish upon a falling moon
There was never any peace
There was never any love or hate
Locking all the lock gates
Shutting it all down
Watching me drown
As my soul never leaves the ground

I can smell the fear
Never can it be clear
I refuse to hear (you)
Silencing all the echoes
Drifting through with no space and time

✿✿✿

STARS

Wishful thinking
On every fallen star
Just to hide out ever
Unfaithful deceiving lies
Spiraling deep in the mind
Of the widows left,
To the devouring shadows

Reach for the falling sky
To catch the hope of the stars
Burning inside of our failing hearts
Just to return to the start
Racing to find the answers
Of the questions that are
Already known

Wishful thinking
To the dying stars
For a life of unwavering
Torment plaguing the fading souls
We hide so well
Beneath our unfaithful scars
To the betraying angels of light

Reach for the falling sky
To catch the hope of the stars
Burning inside of our failing hearts
Just to return to the start
Racing to find the answers
Of the questions that are
Already known
Wishful thinking
To the newborn stars
In hopes of a better life
To break free of our,
Binding chains
That constricts us to
Our forbidden crimes

Wishful thinking
To the elder stars
Release me to
My final end
I can no longer
Hide behind my eyes
Holding onto the memories

Reach for the falling sky
To catch the hope of the stars
Burning inside of our failing hearts
Just to return to the start
Racing to find the answers
Of the questions that are
We already know

❊❊❊

TO THE BROKEN OUTCASTS

Broken down and torn apart
Shattered light only becomes the dark
Now tainted, fading of the innocence in your heart
Feeling like it all goes wrong
Nothing is ever right
Left behind, no will to fight
No will to go on

Hold your hand up high
Let me pick you up
I've been down this winding road
You still can reach for the sky
Don't ever say good-bye
Leave your past to die

Burned under the secrets and scars
Losing all your hidden stars
Drowning water fills the sinking car
Death isn't that far
Taking that final breath
Feeling like there's nothing left
No will to go on

Hold your hand up high
Let me pick you up
I've been down this winding road
You still can reach for the sky
Don't ever say good-bye
Leave your past to die

ROHLAN SULVAR

Don't hide behind the shadows
Let the light shine through your windows
Hold onto your shining star
As the darkness fades afar
Healing of your open scars
The innocence may be gone
Your path is free to choose
Have the will to go on

Hold your hand up high
Let me pick you up
I've been down this winding road
You still can reach for the sky
Don't ever say good-bye
Leave your past to die

Hold your hand up high
Let me pick you up
I've been down this winding road
You still can reach for the sky
Don't ever say good-bye
Leave your past to die

❋❋❋

DREAMS OF MEMORIES

I can smell you
In the winds
Everything that was true
Coming from within
I've done everything I can do
Just to breathe you in

Why do we fade?
From our memories
Every time I run away
From the tragedies
Night into day
My heart begins to sway
To the falling cascades

Empty and hollow
Into your darkness
I begin to follow
Leaving me breathless
Truth is hard to swallow
Give me time to rest

I can see it in your eyes
Remember all the pain
True path where it lies
Blood and sweat to gain
Don't you dare to cry
Slitting deep into my veins

I broke your heart
When it came apart
Shots fired in the dark
Blood spills across the park

Why do we fade?
From our memories
Every time I run away
From the tragedies
Night into day
My heart begins to sway
To the falling cascades

I lay you down
Unto the ground
Head spinning around
Into the dark waters I drown
Your heart my soul
Are bound
When we disappear
Everything will become so clear
I'm always here
For you my dear

Why do we fade?
From our memories
Every time I run away
From the tragedies
Night into day
My heart begins to sway
To the falling cascades

✿✿✿

ARE YOU THERE?

I'm looking up
Beyond the stars
With my eyes
Through my bleeding scars
To the Milky Way
Only our dreams begin to fade

With my screams
Began echoing
Through the silent night
Beyond the realm of dreams
Can you hear me calling?
Towards the light

Without you here
My emotions become unclear
Through the pain
I chose to stay
While you ran away
What was to gain?
Am I going insane?

With my screams
Began echoing
Through the silent night
Beyond the realm of dreams
Can you hear me calling?
Towards the light

Here I go
Into this black hole
Searching for a lost soul
Why did you leave?
I couldn't see that,
I was becoming the enemy
Losing all my energy
Through your agony

With my screams
Began echoing
Through the silent night
Beyond the realm of dreams
Can you hear me calling?
Towards the light

With my screams
Began echoing
Through the silent night
Beyond the realm of dreams

Can you hear me calling?
Towards the light

❀❀❀

BECOMING COLD FROM WORDS

Behind your dead eyes
Beyond the true lies
I've long said my good-byes
Already dead inside
Roll the dice
I'm becoming cold as ice
Broken heart turns black
Fallen apart with the knife in my back
A soul you began to lack
Without a spine
Frozen in time
Will you ever be fine
Dare to walk your line
I've left everyone behind
Falling through a black hole
Never to be whole
Looking for my sever soul
Never to be told
Can you behold
A price for beauty sold
Laughing as you fold
I watch standing alone
I'm on my own
Never able to go home
Behind my back
Never to my face
I'm running in place
Fall behind in your race
So much strife
Filled by the agony
End my life
Becoming the enemy

Take the knife
End these memories
So long old friend
I'll see you at the end
Where the roads will bend
But hearts never mend
Listening to the wind
Is this a dream or is it real?
I have nothing left to feel
When you're not here
What is that you fear?
Beyond the wants and needs
You fail to see
What's inside me
Failing to be
Fading the light
Stray from the fight
Whatever is wrong or right
Disappearing into the shadows of the night

✿ ✿ ✿

WHAT I'VE DONE TO YOU

The blood inside of me
Blind to see
Who I came to be
Failing the need
Just to do the deed

I've left you behind
Alone to walk the line
Questions and answers to find
We will never be fine
You will never be mine
Left alone in my mind

Laughing on the outside
Crying hard on the inside
Places to hide
Racing against the tide
No need to lie
With arms open wide
With no forgiveness to my pride

I can see the sorrow
Hoping for tomorrow
To be better
A life cannot be borrowed
When we feel so hollow
Everything becomes hard to swallow
To be just a lonely follower

Candies and flowers
Could never wash away the fading hours
Times in the showers
Of our memories
Becomes my tragedies
Not worth remembering
Everything we used to be

I won't pretend
On how you feel
Songs can never mend
What became so real
Became so unbendable
Lost within our own fables

Fighting to win
Against my sins
Looking from within
Screams echo in the wind
Floating dreams
It's never as it seems
I'm trying to hold on
But now your gone
Alone and broken
My scars are open

I begin to fade
Now that your gone away
My dreams won't stay
In this bed I lay
The damages have been made
Drifting along this never-ending cascade

✿✿✿

FORGET ME

I'm hypnotized
By the beauty in your eyes
Becoming so paralyzed
By the songs of your lullabies
Hidden behind the lies

Everybody dies
Everybody cries
Through the pain do we realize
That we must sever our ties
This pain won't ever last
Once we let go of the past
Fall through the night
Burning by the light
I have no fight
Blinded by the sight
Devour by our blight

No longer can I feel
Cannot tell if I'm fake or real
Why do I disappear?
Transmissions coming in unclear
I am no longer here
This is it my dear

Everybody dies
Everybody cries
Through the pain do we realize
That we must sever our ties
This pain won't ever last
Once we let go of the past
So here I stand
Fading into the sand
Spread out across the land
Quickly take my hand
Where my soul is banned

Wounds and scars begin to open
I will never be broken
I will not be taken
Just to be forsaken
When we become shaken

To the heart
I began to fall apart
From your shot to the dark
Buried underground
These shadows haunt me now
Creeping with no sound
By these chains that I am bound
Nowhere to be found

Everybody dies
Everybody cries
Through the pain do we realize
That we must sever our ties
This pain won't ever last
Once we let go of the past

THE LIGHT AND DARK OF MY MIND

Just to leave behind
These memories upon the line
Truths left to find
I'm running out of time
Taking back what's truly mine
Questions burned into our minds

Now I fade
To the grey
Where my nightmares lay
And the angels sway
To where I stay
Far into the bay
Forget me and what I say

Everybody dies
Everybody cries
Through the pain do we realize
That we must sever our ties
This pain won't ever last
Once we let go of the past

✿✿✿

ROHLAN SULVAR

INTO THE BEYOND
BELOW TO THE ABYSS

As we lay here
The sky becomes so clear
Without a care and no fear
Wipe away all our tears
Nothing is set in stone
Or laid in concrete
You were never alone
Shackled at your feet
We are free
To be who we need

Skipping rocks at the pond
We look into the great beyond
We held onto our only love
We begin to fly
Into the night
Chasing that fading light
This will be our greatest flight

Bury it all in the sands
Running out of time
Take my hand
We won't be left behind
Run across this desert land
Just to find
What was lost in our minds?
For what kind of man
Am I

THE LIGHT AND DARK OF MY MIND

So dark and demented
I was left tormented
Tainted and shattered
What does it matter?
Batter and broken
My wounds and scars left open
In my dreams
We scream
Echoing through our minds

Dreams and nightmares
Into this agony of abyss
Reaching for our beyond
Only to be scared
Taking only what I dare
Losing myself in this nothingness
Only to die
Watching it through your eyes
No truths and no lies
No tears to cry
I won't say good-bye

We run away
Before we fade
Only our love will stay
Feelings will sway
For every turn
Our fire burns
Floating hearts
Become torn apart
It was never meant to last
In the dark
Feelings so high, disappearing into the dust

✿ ✿ ✿

LUST OR LOVE IN YOUR EYES

Since the first day we met
I've placed my bet
To a path that was never set
But the look in your eyes
Told of desires
No truth, only lies
As you slowly die
Your beating heart was never alive

Was it love?
That shot us high above
As we touch our warmth
Beating hearts of emotions
As we told a tale
In the back of the trail
Burning desires of wanting arise
Lust was truth in disguised

The high of it all
When we took off
Through the night
Soaring high into the flight
Remembering your taste
Never letting it go to waste

Fall beyond the lines
Where did it begin?
Wasting away the time
With our demons within
Leaving it all behind
Living in our sins
In the alley way

THE LIGHT AND DARK OF MY MIND

Feelings and emotions sway
Our means echoing across the star ways
Memories of the burning screams
Have tainted my dreams
None it's gone away
Becoming shattered
Realizing that I never mattered

My heart ripped out
Along with the doubt
Fell into the game
Accepting the shame
But you're to blame

Was it love?
That shot us high above
As we touch our warmth
Beating hearts of emotions
As we told a tale
In the back of the trail
Burning desires of wanting arise
Lust was truth in disguised

You were a beauty to behold
A song to be told
Never to bend or fold
But your soul was sold

✿✿✿

ROHLAN SULVAR

FALLEN

I've fallen
I've fallen
Into sleep
Cutting in too deep
Taking the life, I cannot keep

Tormented pain
For nothing gain
The blood seeps through my veins
And I'm lying here
In my own fears

I slowly drift away
Far from this place
My memories begin to fade
As they slowly stray
Thoughts of being betrayed
Burns into my body
Watch it decay

Tormented pain
For nothing gain
The blood seeps through my veins
And I'm lying here
In my own fears

THE LIGHT AND DARK OF MY MIND

Why do I feel so down?
Slowly losing the sound
Twist my words around
As you bury me into the ground
I won't be bound
Chained up like your hound

Drink for tomorrow
The day is gone
Drink away my sorrow
It won't be long
Pray from dusk till dawn
Singing a broken song

Tormented pain
For nothing gain
The blood seeps through my veins
And I'm lying here
In my own fears

Tormented pain
For nothing gain
The blood seeps through my veins
And I'm lying here
In my own fears

✿✿✿

BROKEN WORDS

Realize
Dead inside
Trying to hide
Watching the tide
Fly away

To a place
So, no one can
See your face
From broken dreams and thoughts
I cannot be bought
Drink away your pain
Digging the needles into the veins
What are you trying to gain?

Drinking lies
Fill our eyes
As the world dies
So, roll the dice
But don't think twice
Won't be the sacrifice
Fly away

THE LIGHT AND DARK OF MY MIND

To a place
So, no one can
See your face
From broken dreams and thoughts
I cannot be bought
Drink away your pain
Digging the needles into the veins
What are you trying to gain?
Living sin
Across the wind
Empty from within
Let it begin
To start over again
Dying of our kin

Won't be left behind
So, let it shine
Tonight, we dine
On what's divine
Break through your mind
To try and find
What belongs to me
So, let it be

To a place
So, no one can
See your face
From broken dreams and thoughts
I cannot be bought
Drink away your pain
Digging the needles into the veins
What are you trying to gain?

ROHLAN SULVAR

Break my sword and shield
I shall never yield
Never to stop
Just to make it to the top

✿✿✿

WORDS OF A DYING SIN

Dragging my soul away
My friendships slowly fade
Why am I drifting so far away?
Slowly being taken
This world has you forsaken

Sleeping, drinking
Everything disappears
Your pain burns in me
Becoming blind to see
Destroying this to be

Growing to be deceased
Every ounce to increased
Burn me alive
And watch me slowly die
Nightmares haunting
Awaken to sleep again

Sleeping, drinking
Everything disappears
Your pain burns in me
Becoming blind to see
Destroying this to be

I laugh in grins
Dying for my sins
Wrap me in tins
Melting me to scream
Echoing through the nightmares of dreams

ROHLAN SULVAR

Bury me down
Far underground
Screams without a sound
To meanings that
No answers were found
No air, dare I start to drown

Sleeping, drinking
Everything disappears
Your pain burns in me
Becoming blind to see
Destroying this to be

Sleeping, drinking
Everything disappears
Your pain burns in me
Becoming blind to see
Destroying this to be

✿✿✿

FRIENDS OF DREAMS AND REALITY

Cry in sorrow
Losing for tomorrow
Can you make it on your own?
Left behind and alone
Inside your home

Take my hand
It'll be alright
Falling time in the sands
Don't ever lose sight
Drifting off this land

Your names on the slate
Your life they're trying to take
This courage you did not make
Scared and shaken, you run
Everything under the burning sun
Do you dare grab the gun?

Take my hand
It'll be alright
Falling time in the sands
Don't ever lose sight
Drifting off this land

Slowly you begin to fade
Into the darkness
Taken you away
Feeling so lifeless
Do you dare to stay?

Take my hand
It'll be alright
Falling time in the sands
Don't ever lose sight
Drifting off this land

Take my hand
It'll be alright
Falling time in the sands
Don't ever lose sight
Drifting off this land

I'm here for you
These words I say
Are true
Everything I can do
Lies within the love
Of the friends
In my dreams and reality

✿✿✿

FORBIDDEN YOU

Silent screams
Have haunted my dreams
The scent you left behind
For me to find
It's flooding my fragile mind

Now I
Now I crave you
Just to get a taste
Of your sweet juices
Just to breathe you in
How can this all be a sin?

This can't be real?
By the touch of
Your skin feels
I'm holding in my fears
Holding back my tears
When you get so near

Now I
Now I crave you
Just to get a taste
Of your sweet juices
Just to breathe you in
How can this all be a sin?

Haunting my dreams
Images of you
Can this be true
Pleasures of pain, screams
Running through my veins
Just to make love to you
In the pouring rain
Passions to gain

Memories of you
This just won't do
So naked and beautiful
I'm not that wonderful
Why do you plague me?
Blinded to see
That you're sucking the life out of me!

Now I
Now I crave you
Just to get a taste
Of your sweet juices
Just to breathe you in
How can this all be a sin?

Now I
Now I crave you
Just to get a taste
Of your sweet juices
Just to breathe you in
How can this all be a sin?

Just to hold you
To make it true

✿✿✿

TO DIE FOR EMPTINESS

Look beyond my eyes
You won't see the lies
Out truth before we die
I'm truly not alive
Watch me disappear into the sky

Stop this torture
Bury me deep into the future
You can't capture me
Falling away
Watch me fade

I'm not who you want me to be
I'm not the one who's blind
I won't be the one who gets left behind
Get out of my mind
The answers you shall not find
I can't be divine

Stop this torture
Bury me deep into the future
You can't capture me
Falling away
Watch me fade

I don't think I can do this anymore
I don't want to be who I was before
Close the door
Lock me in
This is your sin

I'm not afraid of my fears

ROHLAN SULVAR

I won't shed my tears
Can you hear… me
This dream isn't real
Time won't heal
Your broken heart
You're falling apart

Stop this torture
Bury me deep into the future
You can't capture me
Falling away
Watch me fade

Stop this torture
Bury me deep into the future
You can't capture me
Falling away
Watch me fade

✿✿✿

TORMENTED MINDS

Grab the knife
Just to end this life
Filled with suicide
Dead inside
Can't decide
To live or die

Mind of sorrow
Can't live for tomorrow
Pain of screams
Echoing in the dreams
Rivers of blood fills
The empty streams

Swim away
Just to drown
Get away
From the sound
Buried beneath the ground
It won't be found

Mind of sorrow
Can't live for tomorrow
Pain of screams
Echoing in the dreams
Rivers of blood fills
The empty streams

Can this be true
How can this do
Little too few
Drink it all away
Just too slowly fade

The betrayal is real
Broken we feel
Digging into the skull
With something dull
Bury it deep
As they fall asleep

Sitting in the darkness
Hands on your face crying
As the people lying
Wanting to die

Mind of sorrow
Can't live for tomorrow
Pain of screams
Echoing in the dreams
Rivers of blood fills
The empty streams

Mind of sorrow
Can't live for tomorrow
Pain of screams
Echoing in the dreams
Rivers of blood fills
The empty streams

❀❀❀

A DAY GONE WRONG

Feel so dead inside
As I'm shedding my tears
Run and hide
From my fears
Failed to obey
Rotting with decay

Broken down again
Forgetting where to begin
Left alone with my sins
And I'm drinking again

I wanna drown my sorrows
Just to leave my pain behind
Move on for tomorrow
I won't be blind
Can't lose my mind… again

This pain breaks my head
As I paint my eyes red
Never to lay in my own bed
Broken down and left for dead

I wanna drown my sorrows
Just to leave my pain behind
Move on for tomorrow
I won't be blind
Can't lose my mind… again

ROHLAN SULVAR

Why do you tell me lies?
I can see the truth in your eyes
Secretly saying good-bye
This is not your time
And you claim to be my friend
When you show me the end
How could I have let you in?

Slept for so long
Awoke to your song
And now that you're gone
I'm on my own

I wanna drown my sorrows
Just to leave my pain behind
Move on for tomorrow
I won't be blind
Can't lose my mind… again

I wanna drown my sorrows
Just to leave my pain behind
Move on for tomorrow
I won't be blind
Can't lose my mind… again

✿✿✿

DAMAGED SOUL

Another full moon sets in behind
Another night comes setting in
I can feel the chills
As the winds come echoing
Numb to my emotions
I can see what I'm becoming
I can see what you've done to me

I pour another empty glass
As the hours pass me bye
I see the anger rising
As my heart is breaking
Just to mend a damage soul
Looking at my reflection
My mind begins to fold

I sit down to let my darkness
Take me in
Falling away from your grace
Taking up space
Reliving all my pain and sin
Just to let your venom words
Creep beneath my skin
I can hear your voice
Haunting me

I pour another empty glass
As the hours pass me bye
I see the anger rising
As my heart is breaking
Just to mend a damage soul
Looking at my reflection
My mind begins to fold

I hear the screams echoing
Coming from behind
Staring beyond the horizons
Contemplating to cross the line
As I hold the knife
Bloody and beaten
As your venomous words
Speak its sins
I cut my wrists again

I pour another empty glass
As the hours pass me bye
I see the anger rising
As my heart is breaking
Just to mend a damage soul
Looking at my reflection
My mind begins to fold

I pour another empty glass
As the hours pass me bye
I see the anger rising
As my heart is breaking
Just to mend a damage soul
Looking at my reflection
My mind begins to fold

❄❄❄

SILENCE

Venom and poison
Run through my veins
You're empty heart
You're dead
You're dead to me
I am not yours
To control

I remember when
I was so mesmerized
By your beauty
You had me paralyzed
By your sweet words
Froze in time
Before I realized
The reality of it all

I scream out in silence
Just to hold back
My echoes of violence
But the anger in my eyes
Won't let me walk away
Till the blood has spilled
Filled and satisfy
For my pride

I remember when
I was so mesmerized
By your beauty
You had me paralyzed
By your sweet words
Froze in time
Before I realized
The reality of it all

I've lost my heart
I've lost my mind
To the torments of time
Forcing me to walk your line

✿✿✿

EMOTIONS, MY DEPRESSION

Broken and down
I lay awake
In my bed alone
Thoughts of memories
You once again
Haunt my day dreams
And now I...

Drink myself
To stay awake
To stray away
From the emotions
Of my depression
When it leads me
To you

I take blame
For who I've become
For letting you
Do this to me
Destroying everything I
Was meant to be
The future
Was mine to see
And now I...

Drink myself
To stay awake
To stray away
From the emotions
Of my depression
When it leads
To you

It's 3 AM
I've done all
I can
To sever the ties
You still hold on me
In my mind

I'm trying to be fine
Inhaling the lines
Off road to the sidewalks
Filled with chalks of white
Everything about you
Was never alight
And now I...

(X2)
Drink myself
To stay awake
To stray away
From the emotions
Of my depression
When it leads me
To you

✲✲✲

THE FEELINGS ON HIGH

Whisper my name
In the dark
As over our body
Emotions set on fire
As we draw blood
From the pain and pleasure
Your dripping flesh
Forever will I treasure
Your scent lingers
Within my mind
Haunts my dreams
My soul rages
From the desire
That you spark
Rises higher
Damages of the wreckages
From the severe storm
Created through our lust and love
As we dive in head first
For our juices do we thirst
Soak me till I drown
Screams of pleasures
Keep me going hard
Straddle me
Take all of me in
Until I explode
In your mouth
As I scream out
Your name
Rock back and forth
As I slide my tongue north

✿✿✿

FORGOTTEN

Stare up to the hazy sky
As the clouds of smoke drift
Passes by the world
From dusk till dawn
Hypnotized
By the dancing
Of the stars
Lost within time
To forever wonder
The void of space
Make haste
To find your end
So long my friend
Now that your trapped in
My lullabies
As your body becomes paralyzed
Forever mine
Forever forgotten

✿✿✿

UNSPOKEN LOVE

Your beauty radiates
Beyond the brightness flows
Guiding through the darkness
To your ever glow
I can feel your passion
In your heart
The fire burning deep
In your eyes
I've felt the heat of your love
As we embrace
For a taste
Of a forbidden kiss
Just to hold each other
In a state of serenity
A cause of bliss to ecstasy
Twirling to become
An ascending fantasy
A place of your heavens
To the burning passionate desires
The love you give
From a broken and shattered
Heart and soul
Is on to be admired
When you breathe out
I breathe you in, hold you in
Never wanting to let you go
Becoming so mesmerized
To your ability to paralyzed... me
As your beautiful body sways
To your siren's lullabies
Forever on my mind

❀❀❀

LIES OF WEB

I fell for your web of lies
I felt the venom in what you spoke
Spinning to the tears you cried
Voices in my head
Cry out loud
To your unfaithful heart's desire
Devouring until I expire

You
Struggling to remain
The center of attention
Speak your cruel intentions
Cast your spells of false love
There was never any hope
To the path of your forbidden fruit
To become the bittersweet naïve

Shattering my open mind
Beat me down
Bruised and battered
Tearing open my mending soul
My heart is running out of time
You were never fully mine

You
Struggling to remain
The center of attention
Speak your cruel intentions
Cast your spells of false love
There was never any hope
To the path of your forbidden fruit
To become the bittersweet naïve

THE LIGHT AND DARK OF MY MIND

Your deceiving lies spoken
For me to fear all others
I inhale your venom
Misleading the evidence
Failing to see this is you

Your web of lies
Once invincible
Is slowly becoming thin
Too bold and proud
To cry for help
Your cruel intentions
Of false love and hope

You
Struggling to remain
The center of attention
Speak your cruel intentions
Cast your spells of false love
There was never any hope
To the path of your forbidden fruit
To become the bittersweet naïve

❂❂❂

COVER UP THE TRUTH

MY!!
Peace of mind
Now lost to time
You never were mine
Once again, I came out
In second place
Floating away in space
Losing a never winning race

I've just become
A cover for your story
To cover up
Your true intentions
You were a beauty
That fell from grace

UNDO!!!!
My mending heart
Damaging my torn soul apart
Pick apart my failing mind
And when I go astray
Reboot me when
My heartstrings come undone
I've become your mindless fool

I've just been
A cover for your story
Just to cover up your
True love affair
You are no longer
No longer the beauty
That fell from grace

THE LIGHT AND DARK OF MY MIND

I have become numb
To your venomous charm
I won't hear
What broken words you
Chose to speak
Just face it
I want you to fade away
Far from me

Walk away
Disappear to fade
Become the very shade
You always wanted to be
Unknowingly I realized
I never loved you

I've just been
A cover for your
True love affair
You are
You are
You are no longer
No longer that beauty
That fell from grace

✿✿✿

ROHLAN SULVAR

THE MAN IN RED

Emotions, bearing their weight
Holds me down, collapsing
Pain and suffering I endure
Just to make it through the day
I breathe out
Holding in all my doubt
Wandering the world
In my mind
To the answers I cannot find
For love and peace
I look to you

For all the pain and suffering
That I caused
By my uncontrolled actions
I shut myself away
To escape my undoubted guilt
Just to wish that I slip into the fade
To throw away my dreams and memories

But I am, I am
Haunted by my unescapable past
Of my brothers' sins
The demons that follow me
I fail to see
To look within
For who I really need to be
All because of you

For all the pain and suffering
That I caused
By my uncontrolled actions
I shut myself away
To escape my undoubted guilt
Just to wish that I slip into the fade
To throw away my dreams and memories

The sparks in your eyes
When you chose forgiveness
Seeing past all my sins
Embracing you in
So, I'll never forget
What it feels like to hold
I'm just a man in red
With a high price above my head

For all the pain and suffering
That I caused
By my uncontrolled actions
I shut myself away
To escape my undoubted guilt
Just to wish that I slip into the fade
To throw away my dreams and memories

For all the pain and suffering
That I caused
By my uncontrolled actions
I shut myself away
To escape my undoubted guilt
Just to wish that I slip into the fade
To throw away my dreams and memories

✿✿✿

BREAK THE BINDS

Come down from your cloud
Fade away with me
Escape the foul
Embrace my pain and suffering
Leaving a bittersweet taste lingering
Drift away
Come what may
Crash our hearts
On the bay
As the world falls apart
Break the binds
That chain our spinning minds
Just to snort the lines
Tasting our freedom
Jolting from the electro lights
As our souls take flight
Becoming just another blight
In my reflection sight
Lost in the dark
Cut and bleed me
With your words so sharp
It's so playful when you demonized
I've become so mesmerized
By your tainted eyes
You have me so paralyzed
Listening to your repeated broken lies
Nothing is wrong, everything is fine
Becoming willing and able
Drowning to my demons' fable
Cashing in under the table
Leaving me behind

✿✿✿

REMEMBER THE PAIN

Dissolve the sympathy
With the eulogy
Focusing the energy
Of the fallen and lost souls
Of a time long forgotten

Chanting the songs
Just to remember the pain
Bring forth my demons
So, I can continue my suffering
As I'm being devour by my own darkness

Save me, save me
From drowning in my white room
Spinning and spiraling
Shattering what's left
Of my breaking mind
Echoes of my mending soul
I never was unbreakable
Bending my will
Just to silence my standing still

Chanting the songs
Just to remember the pain
Bring forth my demons
So, I can continue my suffering
As I'm being devour by my own darkness

ROHLAN SULVAR

Living in constant fear
Where no one can hear… me
The lines of reality
Aren't so clear
It's getting to be a lot to bear
As I laugh pulling out my hair
Temptation, cross the line
End the life of the living mind
To the ones who get left behind

Chanting the songs
Just to remember the pain
Bring forth my demons
So, I can continue my suffering
As I'm being devour by my own darkness

Dissolve the sympathy
With the eulogy
Focusing all the energy
Of the fallen and lost souls
For the time long forgotten

❀ ❀ ❀

THE PAIN

Bleed me slowly
Let it flow freely
Take it all from me
Leave me to die
But don't you dare
Begin to cry

Cast me away
To where the shadows fade
To where time can be made
To obey or to disobey
Breaking to the fray
Keeping the demons at the bay

Body numb and steady
I wasn't truly ready
To sway to your melody
Holding me down
Just to steal the crown
Buried so far underground
I slowly drown
By false love and truths
I can no longer feel anything
For you

I was paralyzed
By your seducing lullabies
Became so mesmerized
By the beauty of your words
Blinded by your tainted visions
Of your haunting nightmares
Screams of silence

ROHLAN SULVAR

Dreams of raging violence
Echoes through my veins
I can no longer
Endure the pain

The building agony
Of the fading suffering
Only begins to bring
The devouring darkness
I cry out
For fear of doubt
No one can hear
The visions becoming
Scattering and unclear

Release me
From these chains
Inside my brain
Keep me from being insane
As you

Bleed me slowly
Let it flow freely
Take it all from me
Leave me to die
But don't you dare
Begin to cry!

✿✿✿

TRUTH ABOUT ME

Where do I begin?
Maybe I should confess my sins?
How should I start?
I know the truth
Laugh and fall apart
I don't have a heart
I prefer the shadows of the dark
I'm no one's friend
You all will hate me at the end
Don't be sly
Don't try to lie
I'm running out of time

Trust me I know
I'm a fucking prick
I'm just worthless spic
I'm a real piece of shit
I got a small dick
Just to be the asshole bad guy
I'm just fat bitch
You all think
This is a cry for attention
I'll take this to my grave
No one ever appreciated
All I gave

I'm only nice when I want something
I only like to manipulate those I love
Who am I kidding
I'm just a bad joke
Who people wanted to choke
My imaginary friends wish me dead
I'm only amazing in my head
Seeing red
I'm a fake
A pretender
Here's my white flag
I surrender!
Go ahead and get mad
I'm no ones all they ever had
Whatever, I'm not even sad
If you think I'm serious
Dive into my mind
I don't care if I cross the lines
I'm fine
Go ahead and leave me behind

I don't honestly care
On how you feel
Here, let me get you a beer
So, I get this clear
Let me get a pad and pen
Just to hear
I'll open my ear

✿ ✿ ✿

EULOGY TO MYSELF

What can be said?
That hasn't already been said
He had very little friends
That were true and real with him
Everyone else were just acquaintances
They had little care for him
Not really a tragic story
Or sad to see him go the way he did
Probably for the best
That he ended his life
Only a small handful
Will truly miss him
But it won't be for long
Life will move on
I was planning on making this
A long one
But in the same sense, I don't care
No one else does, then I won't
I would wish him the best
But he was a pest

✿✿✿

MY FINAL WORDS

I have done my best
To be a decent friend
But in the end, the end
I have failed your test
And just like the rest
I've been casted aside
Like a shadow
Of an unwanted ghost
I've become a pest
And it tears me up inside

I use to lie awake
Wondering if I was a fake
I couldn't deal with the shaking
My mind is slowly breaking
As I'm left for the taking
To the demons of their shadows
Cracking the windows
Of my failing mind
It was never truly mine

I have done my best
To be a decent friend
But in the end, the end
I have failed your test
And just like the rest
I've been casted aside
Like a shadow
Of an unwanted ghost
I've become a pest
And it tears me up inside
I've tried

THE LIGHT AND DARK OF MY MIND

I've tried to run away
From all of my pain
Throw my soul to the fray
For I will disobey
Drink till my heart
Slowly fades
Just to wish it all away
What was there to gain
Taking it all in vane
I've become their bane

Haunted by the answers found
Forever to be unbound
Beat me till the blood runs out
Without a shadow of a doubt
Left forsaken buried underground

I have done my best
To be a decent friend
But in the end, the end
I have failed your test
And just like the rest
I've been casted aside
Like a shadow
Of an unwanted ghost
I've become a pest
And it tears me up inside

I give you my final words
Left to be only spoken
Just to be heard

✿✿✿

CENTER

Hold onto peace of mind
To find your light
That shines within
Your burning soul
To feel the passion
That dwells within
Your healing heart

Center your body whole
To break free
Of the chains
They've bind you with
Embrace the rage
That's building from
Inside your darkest shadow
Break through the windows
In your mind

Hold onto peace of mind
To find your light
As you make way
Through your devouring darkness
Fight, don't you
Dare take flight
You can end this blight
For you're a gift
No curse can force
You to drown

THE LIGHT AND DARK OF MY MIND

Center your body whole
To break free
Of the chains
They've bind you with
Embrace the rage
That's building from
Inside your darkest shadow
Break through the windows
In your mind

✿✿✿

FLOAT AWAY

Float away
To the setting sun
Float away
Till the world is gone
Trapped between
Fantasy and reality
Ever long
But here I'll stay
Till the memories
Begin to fade
Out of sight
And out of mind
You were not
The answer I came
To find
Forever blind
To the dreams
Of echoing screams
Silence or violence
Nothing is as it seems
Caught in gravities
Tractor beams
Pulling me down
Until I hit the ground
Until my soul slowly drowns

❁ ❁ ❁

Please keep all hands and feet within the cart until it comes to full stop.

Thank you for taking the time to enjoy the ride through my thoughts that are buried within my mind. Once again, feel free to have your opinions on my work and know that I could care less if you hate them and find them not to your liking. I do appreciate those who truly enjoy them to their fullest meanings of entertainment of my suffering.

With best regards,

Rohlan Sulvar

✿✿✿